A picnic with Dad

By Julie Haydon   Photographs by Lyz Turner-Clark

On Saturday,

Dad and I had a picnic

in the park.

In the morning,
we went to a shop
and got some fresh bread.

Dad made ham and egg sandwiches at home.

I put the sandwiches
in a lunch bag.

I put some apples in the bag, too.

Then Dad put two water bottles
in the bag.

It was a hot day.

Dad put an ice pack

in the lunch bag.

The ice pack kept the food cold.

We rode our bikes to the park.
Dad had the lunch bag
in his backpack.

We had our picnic under a big tree.

I liked the ham and egg sandwiches.

Our picnic at the park was good fun.

PM writing

PM Levelled Exemplar Text

Levels 11/12

Recount

Developed specifically for Guided Writing
and Independent Reading

ISBN-13: 978-0-17-013231-2
ISBN-10: 0-17-013231-5

9 780170 132312

ISBN-10 0 17 013205 6 (set)
ISBN-13 978 0 17 013205 3 (set)

NELSON
CENGAGE Learning

For learning solutions, visit cengage.com.au

PM Levels

1
2
3
4
5
6
7
8
9
10
11/12
13
14
15
16
17
18
19
20
21
22
23
24
25

NELSON
CENGAGE Learning™

A Picnic with Dad

Text: Julie Haydon
Series consultant: Annette Smith
Editor: Beth Browne
Design: Mandi Cole
Photographs: Lyz Turner-Clark
Photo Research: Fiona Smith
Production controller: Lisa Porter

Text © 2007 Julie Haydon
Photographs © 2007 Cengage Learning Australia Pty Limited

ISBN 978 0 17 013231 2
ISBN 978 0 17 013205 3 (set)

Cengage Learning Australia
Level 7, 80 Dorcas Street
South Melbourne, Victoria Australia 3205
Phone: 1300 790 853

Cengage Learning New Zealand
Unit 4B Rosedale Office Park
331 Rosedale Road, Albany, North Shore NZ 0632
Phone: 0508 635 766

For learning solutions, visit **cengage.com.au**

Printed in China by 1010 Printing International Ltd
4 5 6 7 8 12 11 10 09

**PM Writing
Blue/Green Level 11/12**

A Picnic with Dad
(Recount)

Flags
(Recount)

Bigger
(Description)

The Angry Bear
(Information Report)

Stop!
(Information Report)

Water from a Tap
(Narrative)

Big Wheels and Little Wheels

Little Wheels

by Annette Smith

Information Report

Big Wheels and Little Wheels

Levels 5/6   Red/Yellow

Key Learning Area   **Technology**

Theme   **How Things Move**

Text Type   *Information Report*

Text Form   **Reference**

Genre   **Non-fiction**

Purpose   **To present information that classifies living or non-living things**

Text Structure

General Statement: Identifies and classifies the subject *(Pages 2–3)*

Description: Provides information about the subject's physical appearance and other characteristics *(Pages 4–15)*

Evaluation: Provides a summary statement about the subject *(Page 16)*

Language Features

- Common nouns *(e.g. wheels, bike, tractor)*
- Pronouns *(e.g. it)*
- Adjectives *(e.g. big, little)*
- Present tense verbs *(e.g. go, goes)*